JOSEPH PRINCE

EATING YOUR WAY TO WHOLENESS

A PRACTICAL GUIDE TO THE HOLY COMMUNION

All Scripture quotations, unless otherwise indicated, are taken from the New King James Version®. Copyright © 1982 by Thomas Nelson, Inc. Used by permission. All rights reserved.

Scripture quotations marked NIV are taken from the Holy Bible, New International Version®, NIV®. Copyright © 1973, 1978, 1984, 2011 by Biblica, Inc. Used by permission of Zondervan. All rights reserved worldwide.

Scripture quotations marked NLT are taken from the Holy Bible, New Living Translation. Copyright © 1996, 2004, 2007, 2013, 2015 by Tyndale House Foundation. Used by permission of Tyndale House Publishers, Inc., Carol Stream, IL 60188. All rights reserved.

Eating Your Way to Wholeness:
A Practical Guide to the Holy Communion
Copyright © 2013
Joseph Prince Ministries
P.O. Box 2115
Fort Mill, SC 29716
USA

Printed in the United States of America
Second edition, first print: December 2017

All rights reserved under International Copyright Law. Contents and/or cover may not be reproduced in whole or in part in any form without the express written consent of the publisher.

INTRODUCTION

I am so glad that you have requested this booklet. As you hold this in your hand, you may be trusting God for healing in a particular area, or simply desiring to walk in a greater measure of physical, mental, and emotional well-being. Well, I want you to know that it is God's heart for you to enjoy divine health and wholeness—in every area of your life. The Bible reveals this so clearly and beautifully in 3 John 1:2:

Beloved, I pray that you may prosper in all things and be in health, just as your soul prospers.

I believe that in this booklet, you will discover how the Holy Communion, also known as the Lord's Supper, is God's divine channel to receiving health and wholeness in your body, mind, and life. And you'll learn to walk in a measure of Jesus' *shalom* like never before!

Like many believers, you may have heard about the Holy Communion, but may not know what the Scriptures really teach about the Lord's Supper.

Perhaps you have some questions about partaking of the Holy Communion.

It's my heart to help answer some of these questions in the pages of this book. I've kept it short and simple so that you can use this as a practical guide when you are partaking of the Holy Communion, and be encouraged to see God's desire for the health and wholeness of you and your loved ones.

My prayer is that you will see the loving heart of our Father expressed through the Holy Communion! May you also discover the power that comes as you receive the blessings of the finished work of Jesus through this covenant meal.

Grace always,

Joseph Prince

THE HOLY COMMUNION

—GOD'S DELIVERY SYSTEM FOR YOUR HEALING AND WHOLENESS

The Holy Communion is God's delivery system by which every good provision and blessing that Christ won for us at the cross is released in our lives.

While they were eating, Jesus took bread, and when he had given thanks, he broke it and gave it to his disciples, saying, "Take and eat; this is my body." Then he took a cup, and when he had given thanks, he gave it to them, saying, "Drink from it, all of you. This is my blood of the covenant, which is poured out for many for the forgiveness of sins."

MATTHEW 26:26–28 NIV

The Holy Communion, also known as the Lord's Supper, is God's delivery system by which every good provision and blessing that Christ won for us at the cross is released in our lives. It is a time of Jesus giving to us, a time of us **receiving** from Him, and a time of enjoying the Lord's love for us through a consciousness of His finished work.

When you pick up the bread, you are holding in your hand the greatest expression of the Lord's love for you. This love made Him subject His body to be beaten, bruised, and broken so that yours can be whole. To eat the bread as you partake of the Holy Communion is to release your faith to receive His health and wholeness in exchange for your sickness and disease.

Likewise, when you drink from the cup, you are reminding yourself that the blood of the sinless Son of God was shed so that you can be forgiven of every failure, fault, and sin, and made forever righteous and blameless in God's sight (see 2 Cor. 5:21). To drink from the cup is to know that you have perfect standing before the Father and that His ears are attentive to your every prayer (see Ps. 34:15).

PARTAKE AND PROCLAIM

JESUS' FINISHED WORK

The Holy Communion is a time of receiving *every* benefit that Jesus died to give you, including healing, wholeness for your mind and body, and provision for every kind of lack.

For I received from the Lord that which I also delivered to you: that the Lord Jesus on the *same* night in which He was betrayed took bread; and when He had given thanks, He broke *it* and said, "Take, eat; this is My body which is broken for you; do this in remembrance of Me." In the same manner *He* also *took* the cup after supper, saying, "This cup is the new covenant in My blood. This do, as often as you drink *it*, in remembrance of Me." For as often as you eat this bread and drink this cup, you proclaim the Lord's death till He comes.

1 CORINTHIANS 11:23–26

The apostle Paul tells us that when we partake of the Holy Communion, we "proclaim the Lord's death till He comes" (1 Cor. 11:26). This means that as a believer, **every time you partake of the Holy Communion, you are declaring—to yourself, to principalities and powers—that the Lord's death and His finished work avail for you.**

You are declaring over your body and your circumstances that through Jesus' death at the cross, you **are**—not trying to be—completely forgiven, eternally righteous, healed, made whole, favored, and protected! You are reminding yourself of all that Jesus has accomplished for you through His perfect finished work.

When you partake of the Holy Communion, I encourage you to take the time to see the Lord's death and finished work availing for you **personally**—His broken body for your healing and health, His shed blood for your complete forgiveness and right standing before God. The Holy Communion then becomes a time of receiving **every** benefit that Jesus died to give you, including healing, wholeness for your mind and body, and provision for every kind of lack.

DISCERN THE LORD'S BODY

—THE BREAD FOR YOUR HEALING

When you eat the bread, God wants you to see the bread as the body of Jesus—stricken, beaten, torn, and broken for your healing and wholeness. This is how you discern the Lord's body when you partake of the Lord's Supper.

. . . who Himself bore our sins in His own body on the tree, that we, having died to sins, might live for righteousness —by whose stripes you were healed.

1 PETER 2:24

Surely He has borne our griefs and carried our sorrows; yet we esteemed Him stricken, smitten by God, and afflicted. But He *was* wounded for our transgressions, *He was* bruised for our iniquities; the chastisement for our peace *was* upon Him, and by His stripes we are healed.

ISAIAH 53:4–5

In order to fully receive God's provision of health and healing, as well as every aspect of His abundant life into our lives, it's important for us to understand what the bread and the cup represent, and to discern the two elements correctly when we partake of the Holy Communion.

First, you need to understand that **the bread represents the body of Christ**. The apostle Paul tells us in 1 Corinthians 11:29–30 that "not discerning the Lord's body" is why many are weak, sickly, and die before their time. So what does it mean to **discern the Lord's body**? It simply means that when you eat the bread, God wants you to see the bread as the body of Jesus—stricken, beaten, torn, and broken for your healing and wholeness.

The next time you hold the bread in your hand, see Jesus at the scourging post. See Him taking the stripes for you. See one stripe after another landing mercilessly on His body for the healing of whatever ailment or sickness is holding your body captive. Tell yourself, "**Surely** He has borne my sicknesses and carried my pains." That is how you discern the Lord's body when you partake of the Lord's Supper. And when you discern the Lord's body like this, you will be strong, healthy, and live long!

THE CUP IS FOR YOUR FORGIVENESS

When
you drink of
the cup,
be conscious
that because
the Son of God
paid the penalty
for your sins,
you have been
completely
forgiven and
made righteous.

In Him we have redemption through His blood, the forgiveness of sins, according to the riches of His grace.

EPHESIANS 1:7

For as by one man's disobedience many were made sinners, so also by one Man's obedience many will be made righteous.

ROMANS 5:19

For He made Him who knew no sin *to be* sin for us, that we might become the righteousness of God in Him.

2 CORINTHIANS 5:21

When we drink of the cup as we receive the Communion, God wants us to do it with the full realization of what the cup represents and what that means for us today.

Beloved, **the cup represents Jesus' blood, shed for the forgiveness of our sins** (see Col. 1:14, Eph. 1:7). Jesus Himself said, "For this is My blood of the new covenant, which is shed for many for the remission of sins" (Matt. 26:28).

So when you drink of the cup, be conscious that because the Son of God paid the penalty for your sins, you have been completely forgiven and made righteous. Partake, rejoicing that the blood of Jesus has given you right standing before God so that you can always come boldly into His presence, and find His grace and mercy to help you at every point of need (see Heb. 4:16)!

A COMMON MISCONCEPTION

God wants us to understand that the Communion is a blessing to be received because of His goodness and Jesus' finished work.

Therefore whoever eats this bread or drinks *this* cup of the Lord in an unworthy manner will be guilty of the body and blood of the Lord. But let a man examine himself, and so let him eat of the bread and drink of the cup. For he who eats and drinks in an unworthy manner eats and drinks judgment to himself. . . . For if we would judge ourselves, we would not be judged.

1 CORINTHIANS 11:27–29, 31

I've heard teachings based on Paul's words in 1 Corinthians 11:28 that say believers have to "examine themselves" before partaking of the Holy Communion, and that only believers who are worthy to partake can partake, lest they incur God's judgment. Sadly, this erroneous teaching has turned something God meant to be a blessing into a curse for many sincere believers.

So what does it mean to "examine" ourselves when we partake of the Lord's Supper? It simply means that we are to examine if we understand that the body of Jesus was broken for our healing, and His blood was shed for the forgiveness of all our sins. It means we are to judge ourselves in the light of Jesus' finished work. We are to see ourselves beloved, forgiven, and qualified by the Lord not only to partake of the Lord's Supper, but also to receive every blessing and benefit of His finished work.

Paul goes on to say that if we so judge ourselves, we will not suffer the curse of aging, degeneration, sickness, and death, which is God's judgment on the earth because of sin (see 1 Cor. 11:31).

God wants us to understand that the Communion is a **blessing to be received** because of His goodness and Jesus' finished work. So instead of looking at **yourself** to see if you have any unconfessed sin or if you are worthy enough, see how the blood of **Jesus** has enabled you to stand boldly before Him today—your sins cleansed, and His righteousness set to your account—to receive healing for your body and provision for every need!

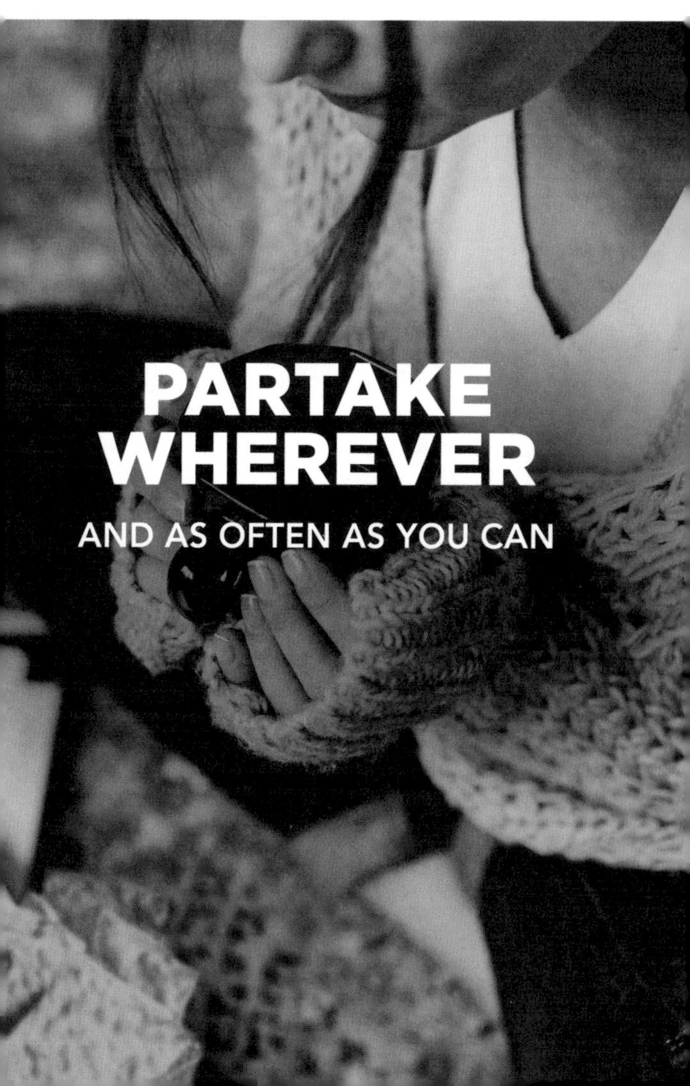
PARTAKE
WHEREVER
AND AS OFTEN AS YOU CAN

Partake as often as you can, and believe that each time you do, you are receiving more and more of Jesus' divine health into your body.

Every day they continued to meet together in the temple courts. They broke bread in their homes and ate together with glad and sincere hearts.

ACTS 2:46 NIV

A common question I'm asked is, "How often can I partake of the Holy Communion?"

God's Word doesn't tell us how often to partake of the Communion, but if you read the Bible, you'll see that the early church in the book of Acts broke bread (that's the Communion) on a daily basis as they met and went from house to house (see Acts 2:46).

Paul, when talking about partaking of the Lord's Supper, said, "**For as often as you eat this bread and drink this cup**" (1 Cor. 11:26). That means you can take it as often as you feel you need to. And every time you do, you are simply ingesting more and more of Jesus' health and wholeness into your body!

If you are reading this and have been given bad news or a negative report from your doctor, I encourage you to take the Communion the way you would take your medicine. And unlike earthly medications, God's way to healing and health has no side effects, only amazing benefits! So partake as often as you can, and believe that each time you do, you are receiving more and more of Jesus' divine health into your body.

Other questions I'm often asked are, "Can I take it on my own at home?" and "Do I need special bread and drink to constitute the elements?"

Beloved, you can partake of the Holy Communion anywhere—in your personal time with the Lord, with your family before or after a meal, or with fellow believers whenever you gather! What's important to remember is that **the Communion is not a ritual to be observed, but a blessing to be received**.

To prepare the Holy Communion elements, you don't need a prescribed bread or special drink. Jesus, on the night He instituted the Holy Communion, used whatever bread and drink that was available and customarily used at the time. Similarly, all you need to do is get any readily available bread and drink as a point of release for your faith.

LET'S GET STARTED

—PARTAKE YOUR WAY TO WHOLENESS

Right in the presence of our enemies, right in the midst of our symptoms, pains, or lack, God prepares a table—the Communion—before us.

And He took bread, gave thanks and broke *it*, and gave *it* to them, saying, "This is My body which is given for you; do this in remembrance of Me." Likewise He also *took* the cup after supper, saying, "This cup *is* the new covenant in My blood, which is shed for you."

LUKE 22:19–20

You prepare a table before me in the presence of my enemies; You anoint my head with oil; my cup runs over.

PSALM 23:5

Psalm 23:5 tells us that right in the presence of our enemies, right in the midst of our symptoms, pains, or lack, God prepares a table (the Communion) before us. So let's come boldly today to the Lord's table and receive afresh His health, strength, wholeness, and life!

Are you ready to join with me in this covenant meal?

First, hold the bread in your hand and say:

> *"Thank You, Jesus, for Your broken body. Thank You for bearing my symptoms and sicknesses at the cross so that I may have Your health and wholeness. I declare that by Your stripes, by the beatings You bore, by the lashes that fell on Your back, I am completely healed. I believe and I receive Your resurrection life in my body today."*
>
> [Eat.]

Next, take the cup in your hand and say:

> *"Thank You, Jesus, for Your blood that has washed me whiter than snow. Your blood has brought me forgiveness and made me righteous forever. And as I drink, I celebrate and partake of the inheritance of the righteous, which includes preservation, healing, wholeness, and all Your blessings."*
>
> [Drink.]

Hallelujah! Now, as you've just partaken of Jesus' body and blood, be conscious that His strength, healing, divine health, and life are flowing in your veins right now. See His amazing love for you and expect His abundant supply to swallow up every symptom of lack in your circumstances.

Beloved, keep partaking of this powerful covenant meal. The more you partake, the stronger you will become. You will live and not die. You will experience length of days and the abundant life that is yours in Christ! Amen!

• • •

PRAISE
REPORTS

Keep partaking of this powerful covenant meal. The more you partake, the stronger you will become.

**Then Jesus declared,
"I am the bread of life. Whoever comes to me will never go hungry, and whoever believes in me will never be thirsty."**

JOHN 6:35 NIV

"I will give you back your health and heal your wounds," says the Lord.

JEREMIAH 30:17 NLT

Bless the Lord, O my soul, and forget not all His benefits: who forgives all your iniquities, who heals all your diseases.

PSALM 103:2–3

My ministry has received many, many precious testimonies from people who have experienced the blessings of the finished work through partaking of the Holy Communion. I've included some of these here to encourage you. As you read these wonderful praise reports, remember that God is not a respecter of persons—what He has done for these folks, He can also do for you! He is the same, yesterday, today, and forever (see Heb. 13:8), and is always faithful to His Word. May you also experience the goodness and abundant grace of our Lord Jesus!

Holy Communion Brings Amazingly Quick Recovery

NATALIE | MISSOURI, UNITED STATES

I rarely fall ill, but then, I started feeling unwell and my condition got worse by the day. However, I kept going, as being a single mom, I did not have the luxury of taking it easy.

One day, after I had sent my son off to school and was trying to get ready for work, I was in such intense pain and discomfort that I thought I needed to go to the emergency room.

As I had been listening to your teaching on the Holy Communion, the Holy Spirit prompted me to call my friend to partake of the Communion together and pray in agreement with me.

I did just that, and both of us prayed and received the Communion over the phone—she had juice and a cracker and I had juice and a piece of bread. After that, we continued to talk about the Lord and how good He had been to us over the past twenty-four years.

As we continued talking, I suddenly realized that I was laughing and completely healed and restored. My friend was amazed at my quick recovery!

Thank you, Pastor Prince, for being a true and faithful teacher of the Word.

Black Dots in Eye Gone after Communion

WALTER | NEW YORK, UNITED STATES

I have been a born-again Christian since March 11, 1977. Ever since I watched you on TV, I have been hungering for God's Word like never before.

Anyway, I was at work one day and all of a sudden, my right eye went blurry and I saw thousands of black dots. I went to my eye doctor after work and he said that I needed to have emergency surgery on my eye.

Since I had read your book on the Holy Communion previously, I told my doctor that I wanted to wait and not have the surgery. I then partook of the Holy Communion two to three times a day. When I went back for a checkup, a specialist came to have a look at my eye and found zero black spots.

The Lord Jesus is so good. My wife, Pam, and I shared my experience with people and got very odd looks from most of them. We partake of the Holy Communion almost every day. We've never gotten sick ever since we started doing so two and a half years ago. Praise the Lord!

Receiving the Abundance of Grace for Academic Achievements

JADEN | FLORIDA, UNITED STATES

I am very thankful for your ministry! I've learned to apply rest, by the grace of Jesus, instead of my self-efforts, and I've seen awesome results.

When I enrolled in college to get my degree in audio engineering, I started off intimidated because I was in my forties and hadn't been in school for many years. I thought I would have trouble studying and recalling information.

I decided to apply your teachings and not trust in my own strength, but to receive the abundance of grace and believe that I have the mind of Christ. I would receive Communion almost every day before class and partake of Jesus' broken body.

To make a long story short, I just graduated top in my class with a 3.98 out of a possible 4.0 GPA. I was also awarded Perfect Attendance as well as four special awards by different course directors.

It is so liberating to know that I can rest in Christ's finished work and He will always cause me to triumph!

CLOSING WORDS

My friend, partaking of the Holy Communion is not just about healing. It is about remembering the Lord Jesus and receiving the fullness of the blessings that He died on the cross to give you. Beloved, there are so many more benefits that I want to share with you, and I pray that you will find out more about what the Lord has for you.

Here are two unique resources related to receiving God's healing and protection through the Lord's Supper. I hope you will avail yourself of them from my ministry's online store at **JosephPrince.org**:

1.

HEALTH AND WHOLENESS THROUGH THE HOLY COMMUNION
(SOFTBACK BOOK)

2.

HEALTH & WHOLENESS THROUGH THE HOLY COMMUNION
(DVD BOX SET—NTSC)

You can also find out more about the Holy Communion from my ministry's website.

And if you've been blessed by the praise reports shared in this booklet, I believe you'll be greatly encouraged by the many other testimonies my ministry has received from believers who have partaken of the Lord's Supper and experienced the Lord's healing and protection. You can find these in the Praise Reports page online. I pray that as you read them, faith will fill your heart and cause you to look to Jesus for whatever you need when you partake of the Holy Communion.

• • •

Special Appreciation

Special thanks and appreciation to all who have sent in their testimonies and praise reports to us. Kindly note that all testimonies are received in good faith and edited only for brevity and fluency. Names have been changed to protect the writers' privacy.

Salvation Prayer

If you would like to receive all that Jesus has done for you and make Him your Lord and Savior, please pray this prayer:

Lord Jesus, thank You for loving me and dying for me on the cross. Your precious blood washes me clean of every sin. You are my Lord and my Savior, now and forever. I believe You rose from the dead and that You are alive today. Because of Your finished work, I am now a beloved child of God and heaven is my home. Thank You for giving me eternal life and filling my heart with Your peace and joy. Amen.

We Would Like to Hear from You

If you have prayed the salvation prayer or if you have a testimony to share after reading this book, please tell us about it via **JosephPrince.org/praise**. We'd love to hear from you!

Connect with Us

Visit JosephPrince.org today to:

Be Inspired—Sign up for our FREE daily inspirational emails.

Be Encouraged—Read about how the gospel of grace is making a difference one life at a time.

Watch Joseph—Catch his FREE daily broadcast on-demand and receive the gospel of grace anytime, anywhere.

For bite-sized inspirations on-the-go, follow Joseph on:

fb.com/JosephPrince

@JosephPrince

twitter.com/JosephPrince

Other Books by Joseph Prince

Live the Let-Go Life

Grace Revolution

The Prayer of Protection

The Power of Right Believing

Unmerited Favor

Destined to Reign

The Prayer of Protection Devotional

Glorious Grace

Reign in Life

Destined to Reign Devotional

100 Days of Right Believing

100 Days of Favor

Provision Promises

Healing Promises

For more information on these books and other inspiring resources, visit JosephPrince.org.

My Reflections

"For I *am* the LORD who heals you."

EXODUS 15:26

My Reflections

He sent His word and healed them, and delivered *them* from their destructions.

PSALM 107:20